WOMEN IN THE WEST

Rachel Stuckey

PowerKiDS press

Published in 2016 by **The Rosen Publishing Group, Inc.**
29 East 21st Street, New York, NY 10010

Developed and produced for Rosen by BlueAppleWorks Inc.

Art Director: T.J. Choleva
Managing Editor for BlueAppleWorks: Melissa McClellan
Designer: Joshua Avramson
Photo Research: Jane Reid
Editor: Jennifer Way

Illustration & Photo Credits: Cover Joshua Avramson; title page Albert Bierstadt/Public Domain; cover, title page, back cover (skull) Jim Parkin/Shutterstock; cover, title page (wood) Dagmara_K/Shutterstock; back cover background homydesign/Shutterstock; background siro46 /Shutterstock; chapter intro backgrounds rangizzz/Shutterstock; p. 4 Charles M. Russell/Public Domain; p. 7 Edgar Samuel Paxson/Public Domain; p. 8, 16, 22, 26, 28 Everett Historical/Shutterstock; p. 11, 14, 20, 24 Public Domain; p. 12 William Herbert Dunton/Public Domain; p. 15 Paul Frenzeny/Public Domain; p. 18, 19, 21 Carlyn Iverson

Cataloging-in-Publication-Data
Stuckey, Rachel.
Women in the west / by Rachel Stuckey.
p. cm. — (The true history of the Wild West)
Includes index.
ISBN 978-1-4994-1181-2 (pbk.)
ISBN 978-1-4994-1209-3 (6 pack)
ISBN 978-1-4994-1204-8 (library binding)
1. Women pioneers — West (U.S.) — History — 19th century — Juvenile literature. 2. Pioneers — West (U.S.) — History — 19th century — Juvenile literature. 3. Frontier and pioneer life — West (U.S.) — Juvenile literature. I. Stuckey, Rachel II. Title.
F596.S78 2016
978'.02'082—d23

Manufactured in the United States of America

CPSIA Compliance Information: Batch #WS15PK
For Further Information contact: Rosen Publishing, New York, New York at 1-800-237-9932

CONTENTS

Native American women played important roles in their community. They were builders, warriors, farmers, and craftswomen.

Women of the West

The stories we hear about the Wild West are usually about men. It's true that most of the first American settlers to the western **frontier** were men. They were **fur traders**, mountain men, and **miners**. But there were also women and they were very strong and brave. Many women traveled with their families. Other women went west alone looking for freedom and opportunities they could not have in the East.

For more than a century before the Americans came to the West, Spanish settlers had been making their homes in the northern Mexican provinces that are now California, Nevada, Arizona, and New Mexico. The West was also home to thousands of Native Americans with diverse cultures and languages. Women were an important part of both Spanish and Native civilization in the region long before the era of the Wild West.

The Early Frontier

In the early 1700s, the western edge of the thirteen colonies was the first North American frontier. After the American Revolution, American settlers crossed the Appalachian Mountains and settled the land east of the Mississippi River. Women lived difficult lives on the early frontier, and worked hard to build **homesteads** there. There were also conflicts between the French, the British, and the new American government.

The Californios

In the late 1700s and early 1800s, the **Californios**, or Spanish-speaking settlers of California, owned huge ranchos. The Catholic Californios were a mix of Spanish, Native American, and African ancestry. Californios had easy lives on the frontier—good weather, fertile land, and Native Americans to work for them as servants or slaves. Californio women had many children, and their husbands or fathers were in charge of the family. But Californio women also had the right to own and control property under Mexican law, so many became wealthy landowners and owned ranchos on their own.

Sacagawea

Sacagawea was a Shoshone Native American who was born around 1788 in today's Idaho. When she was about 12 years old, she was kidnapped by a group of Hidatsa Native Americans and taken to what is now North Dakota. She was still living among the Hidatsa in 1804, when Meriwether **Lewis** and William **Clark** hired her to work as a translator with her French-Canadian husband. On the expedition to the Pacific Ocean, she translated Native American languages into Hidatsa and her husband translated Hidatsa into French. Sacagawea's most important role in the expedition was being a sign of peace. Sacagawea was a teenager with an infant son. Whenever the expedition met with a new tribe, the presence of Sacagawea and child signaled that the explorers were not warriors. When the expedition reached Shoshone lands, Sacajawea was reunited with her brother, the chief, who provided the expedition with horses. Lewis and Clark were very grateful to Sacagawea. Clark later paid for her son to go to school.

Women worked hard on the frontier. They cared for their husbands and their children as well as the family's farm.

Frontier Women

Life on the frontier was hard work. There were no stores where settlers could buy food or other supplies like clothes or tools. First, they had to clear the land and build their own homes, which were usually one-room cabins. Women were very important in frontier life. They made many of the things the family needed to survive. They grew vegetable gardens and raised chickens, pigs, and cows to help feed the family. The frontier had few doctors, so women also provided medical care to their families and neighbors. Before schools were built, frontier women taught their children to read, write, and work with numbers.

The very first frontier women traveled west with their husbands or fathers in wagon trains. Some women were missionaries. Others settled **land claims** and started farms or ranches with their families.

Women Ranchers

Many women moved west to start farms with their husbands. But ranches were also an important part of the West. Some ranches raised sheep, goats, or even horses, but the biggest ranches were cattle ranches. Women ranchers looked after the home, and also helped run the business of the ranch. Everyone pitched in. Most women ranchers rode horses, rounded up cattle, and shot guns just like the men did. Some women worked as cowgirls, herding cattle and fighting off **cattle rustlers**.

A ranch had many jobs, such as feeding the livestock, milking the cows, cleaning the barn, and tending the garden and hay fields. Many women also managed the accounts, keeping track of the ranch's money and the number of cattle. Women often took over the ranch if their husbands were sick or died.

Cattle Kate

Cattle Kate was an **outlaw** in the West — or was she? She was never violent and she was never charged with any crime. She made the mistake of opposing powerful cattle ranchers in Wyoming.

Cattle Kate's real name was Ellen Watson.

Cattle Kate moved to Wyoming on her own and worked as a seamstress and cook. With the money she earned she bought cattle and started a small ranch. The large cattle ranchers wanted to take over small ranches like hers, but she refused to sell her herd or her land.

In 1889, a powerful rancher accused Cattle Kate of stealing cattle and sent his men to kill her and her husband. The killers were never tried because witnesses were threatened or died. The press published the powerful rancher's story that Cattle Kate was a cattle rustler and not an honest rancher.

Women in the Wild West took on what were traditionally men's roles both out of choice and out of necessity.

Strong Individuals

The American West was settled by strong, brave, hardworking women. Men and women were certainly not equal in Western society though. In addition to any nontraditional work they did, women were still expected to do housework like cooking, cleaning, and taking care of children. But unlike the strict social rules back East, Western society was more open. This openness attracted many independent women to the freedom of the West. There, they were able to make land claims and run their own businesses. Many of these women were forgotten by history. Today, historians have started to tell the stories of less well-known women in the West— describing the work they did and the contributions they made. However, there were also many women who became famous during their own lifetimes and are already an established part of Wild West history.

Little Sure Shot Annie Oakley

Annie Oakley is the most famous woman of the Wild West era and the first American superstar! Her real name was Phoebe Ann Mosey and she was born in 1860 in Ohio. She grew up in a poor family and had to work instead of going to school. She learned to hunt to help feed her family. She also sold her game to shopkeepers and hotels. By the time she was 15, she had earned enough to pay the mortgage on her mother's farm.

One day, a traveling performer named Frank E. Butler challenged the men in town to a shooting competition. He lost to the five-foot-tall Phoebe Ann Mosey! Soon the sharpshooters married and Phoebe Ann Mosey took the stage name of Annie Oakley. Oakley and Butler performed their shooting skills all around the United States.

14

Buffalo Bill (above) was so impressed by Annie Oakley's skills that he featured her in his Wild West show for almost 17 years.

The pair soon joined Buffalo Bill's Wild West Show where Oakley amazed crowds all over the world. Lakota chief Sitting Bull called her Watanya Cicilla, which means "Little Sure Shot." Annie Oakley was such a good shot that she could split a playing card through its edge. She shot apples off her dog's head. While touring Europe and performing for kings and queens, Oakley shot the ashes off the cigarette in the mouth of Kaiser Wilhelm II of Germany.

Here is Calamity Jane standing at the grave of her friend Wild Bill Hickok, in Deadwood, Dakota Territory.

Calamity Jane

Martha "Calamity Jane" Canary was born in 1852 in Missouri. She was the eldest of six children. In 1865, her family moved west by wagon train, but her mother died on the way. Her father died in 1867, and after his death the teenaged Martha Jane took her brothers and sisters to the Wyoming Territory. She did whatever job she could to support her family—dancer, nurse, dishwasher, waitress, cook, and even an ox team driver. In 1874, she started working as a scout for the U.S. Army at Fort Russell. By 1876, she was known by the name Calamity Jane and was traveling with the gunfighter and gambler

MYTH: The life stories and adventures of Calamity Jane are all true.

TRUTH OR MYTH? Calamity Jane was a real person, but most of what we know about her is myth. In the 1870s, the writer of the Deadwood Dick **dime novels** used Jane as a character, but he made up all the stories. People soon confused the real Jane with the Jane in the novels. In the 1890s, Jane worked in Wild West shows as a storyteller and exaggerated her own adventures to entertain the audience. A book written to promote her performances, *The Life and Adventures of Calamity Jane by Herself* is a mix of truth and fiction. Long after Jane died, a woman claiming to be her daughter published letters she said were written by Jane. The letters were probably fake—Jane could barely read and write. We'll never really know the truth about Calamity Jane, one of the biggest legends of the Wild West!

Wild Bill Hickok to Deadwood in present-day South Dakota. Jane was a rough woman who did not fit into polite society. She drank too much alcohol and often behaved badly. But she also was famous for her kindness and generosity. She rescued people in trouble and often nursed the sick.

In Search of Gold

While many settlers headed west to set up farms and ranches, it was mining that really built the West. The first major gold rush in 1848 brought thousands of people to northern California. Later discoveries created **mining towns** in Alaska, Klondike, Colorado, Nevada, and elsewhere. Most miners and **prospectors** were men. Women were an uncommon sight in mining towns. Some miners brought their families, but more often, women in mining towns had come on their own. Women worked in and even owned stores, restaurants, **boarding houses**, laundries, and saloons. Some worked as prospectors, too. These women earned lots of money in the mining towns and invested in property and mining operations. They helped to civilize mining towns by organizing churches, schools, and hospitals.

Nellie Cashman

Nellie Cashman is a well-known frontier woman in both the United States and Canada.

She was born in Ireland in 1845, and grew up in Boston, Massachusetts. She moved west in 1865, where she ran boarding houses and restaurants in different mining towns. During the Klondike Gold Rush in Canada, Cashman led a team to rescue miners trapped in the mountains. She then worked as a nurse and businesswoman in Tombstone, Arizona. She later moved to the Yukon in Alaska to prospect for gold.

Clara Brown

Clara Brown was a former slave who settled in Colorado in 1856, at the age of 56. There she worked as a laundress, a cook, and a midwife, and invested her money in land and mining. She was a leader in her community and well known for helping people. After the Civil War ended in 1865, Brown used her money to help former slaves move west to start new lives. Just before she died in 1885 she was made a member of the Society for Colorado Pioneers.

Gamblers and Outlaws

The Wild West wasn't quite as wild as the movies show, but there were still some less respectable characters. Some were famous for bad behavior like drinking, gambling, and fighting. Others were criminal outlaws. The following women fell into this category either on their own, or because of who they associated with.

Etta Place

Etta Place ran with the outlaws known as Butch Cassidy and the Sundance Kid. No one knows her real name or where she came from. Those who met her said she was pretty, friendly, and educated. She was also a great shot with a rifle. In 1901, she visited Tiffany's jewelry store in New York City with the Sundance Kid and posed for a portrait with him. She later traveled to South America with the outlaws. After Butch and Sundance were killed, Etta Place disappeared from history.

Poker Alice

Alice Ivers was born in England in 1851, and moved to Leadville, Colorado, as a young woman. Her first husband taught her to play **poker**, but he died a few years after they married. Alice started to play poker all over the West. She later worked in saloons as a dealer. She married two more times, but continued playing poker. She often traveled to New York to buy the latest fashions with her winnings.

Lottie Deno

Lottie Deno was a gambler in Texas in the late 1800s. Her real name was Carlotta J. Thompkins and she came to San Antonio as a young woman in 1865. She started working as a **house gambler**. When her husband Frank was accused of murder, the pair left town and traveled through Texas, earning their living by playing poker.

One-room schoolhouses were typical in the Wild West era. There, a single teacher taught several grade levels of children.

Brave Teachers

Thousands of single women moved west to be teachers. Being a teacher was an excellent way for unmarried women to be independent and move away from their families. Some young teachers were even able to hold land claims while they worked as teachers. Most schools in the West were one room and had students of all grade levels. Many teachers were still teenagers and may have been the same age as some of their students.

Being a teacher allowed young women to be on their own, although they usually married after a few years of teaching. Because there were so many men in the West, teachers could often choose from among many suitors. It also meant that schools had to hire new teachers every year or so. By the 1870s, one in four white women in America had worked as a teacher.

Catharine Beecher

Catharine Beecher was born in 1800 in New York. She was part of a famous family of religious leaders and **abolitionists**. Catharine's sister, Harriet Beecher Stowe, wrote the book *Uncle Tom's Cabin*. Beecher was also a writer and an educator. She was committed to the education of women at a time when many people did not think girls could learn difficult subjects like mathematics. She also believed girls should have a physical education and be allowed to exercise instead of sitting quietly at home.

Beecher developed a new approach to teaching and encouraged the training of women to become teachers on the frontier. In addition to opening schools for girls, she started the Ladies' Society for Promoting Education in the West. The society founded teacher colleges in Iowa, Illinois, and Wisconsin.

MYTH: Teenage girls worked as teachers.

TRUTH OR MYTH? This is true. Young women at this time could earn a teaching certificate before even completing high school. Laura Ingalls lived with her family in the Dakota Territory. In the winter of 1882, when she was 15 years old, Ingalls had earned her "third grade" certification and was sent to work as a teacher in a nearby settlement. Ingalls lived with a student's family in their two-room **claim shanty**. She was homesick and had a difficult time with her students. Over the next three years, Ingalls taught in two more schools. In between teaching jobs she attended school herself, but never finished high school. She stopped teaching at the age of 18, after she married Almanzo Wilder. Later in her life, Ingalls Wilder wrote the Little House novels about her life. She describes her work as a teacher in the book *These Happy Golden Years*.

She later started the American Women's Educational Association, which recruited and trained teachers for the west. Hundreds of the best teachers who went west were trained using Catharine's approach.

Here is Colorado governor Oliver H. Shoup in 1919 signing an amendment that will grant all American women the right to vote. Women in Colorado had won the vote in 1893.

Fighting for a Better Future

While women in the West worked hard alongside men and could own property, they were not treated equally as American citizens. Back in the East, the women's suffrage movement had started in the 1840s and was led by activists like Elizabeth Cady Stanton and Susan B. Anthony. Because many people went west seeking greater freedom, western settlers were more open to new ideas about women's role in society. Wyoming passed the first law allowing women to vote in 1869—50 years before the federal law. By the end of the 1800s, women could vote in local and state elections in Wyoming, Utah, Idaho, and Colorado. Washington, California, Oregon, Kansas, and Arizona also gave women the right to vote long before all American women were granted the right to vote in 1920.

Toward the Modern Era

Women were just as much a part of making history and settling the West as men. Farmers, ranchers, miners, businesswomen, nurses, and teachers all helped build the West. While most women in the West still married and took care of the home, they still had more rights, such as owning property and voting. Women also played an important role in civilizing the West. Schools, hospitals, and church organizations run by women helped make life better for settlers in the West.

The opportunity to work and be successful on their own showed that women were strong and capable.

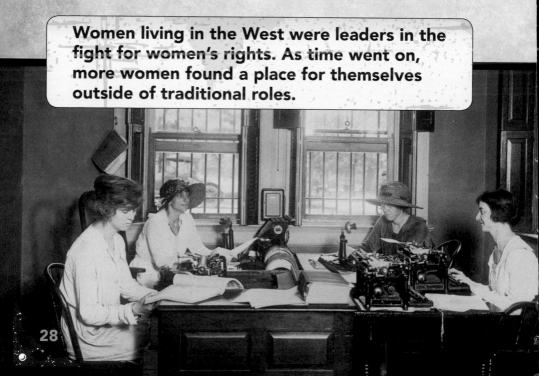

Women living in the West were leaders in the fight for women's rights. As time went on, more women found a place for themselves outside of traditional roles.

Esther Morris was born in 1814 in New York. She trained as a hat maker before she married and started a family. In 1868, her husband and sons went to Wyoming Territory to prospect for gold. Morris joined her family the following year, just as women in the territory were being granted the right to vote. Some of the Wyoming Territory's government officials disagreed with allowing women to vote and quit their jobs in protest. These men had to be replaced quickly to keep order in the territory, and Morris was appointed to take the position of **justice of the peace** for South Pass in 1870. Morris became the first woman justice of the peace in the United States, making her famous and earning her a place in American history.

As the Wild West era ended, the idea that women should be educated, make their own decisions, and take care of themselves became part of American culture. It took many more years for women to gain the rights that they have today, but the women of the Wild West helped lay the foundation of the roles that women play in modern American society.

Glossary

abolitionists People who worked for the abolition, or end, of slavery.

boarding houses Places where people can rent rooms in a large house.

Californios The Spanish-speaking people who lived in California before Americans moved west.

cattle rustler A person who stole cattle on the open range.

claim shanty A small cabin built quickly so a person could live on a piece of land and claim it as their own.

dime novels Short, inexpensive books with exciting stories.

frontier The wilderness at the edge of a territory that hasn't yet been settled.

fur traders Men who trapped animals for their furs and sold them.

homesteads Homes and other buildings and the land those buildings are on.

house gambler A skilled gambler paid by the owner of a casino or saloon who gives the owner a portion of their winnings.

justice of the peace A judge that deals with local crime and legal issues.

land claim A piece of land that is claimed by a settler by marking the land and living on it for a certain amount of time.

Lewis and Clark Leaders of the Corps of Discovery expedition, which traveled from St. Louis to the Pacific Ocean from 1804 to 1806.

miners People who remove metals and gems from the ground.

mining towns Towns that were built very quickly near new mines.

outlaw A person who has broken the law and avoids law enforcement.

poker A card game in which players bet that their cards are the best.

prospector A person who searches for gold or other valuable metals or gems.

For More Information

Further Reading

George-Warren, Holly. *The Cowgirl Way: Hats Off to America's Women of the West.* Boston, MA: HMH Books for Young Readers, 2010.

Norwich, Grace. *I Am Sacagawea.* New York, NY: Scholastic, 2012.

Sanford, William R. and Green, Carl R. *Calamity Jane: Courageous Wild West Woman.* Berkeley Heights, NJ: Enslow Pub Inc, 2012.

Winter, Jonah. *Wild Women of the Wild West.* New York, NY: Holiday House, 2011.

Websites

Due to the changing nature of Internet links, PowerKids Press has developed an online list of websites related to the subject of this book. This site is updated regularly. Please use this link to access the list: www.powerkidslinks.com/tthow/women

Index